YOUR KNOWLEDGE HAS VALUE

- We will publish your bachelor's and
  master's thesis, essays and papers

- Your own eBook and book -
  sold worldwide in all relevant shops

- Earn money with each sale

Upload your text at www.GRIN.com
and publish for free

Bibliographic information published by the German National Library:

The German National Library lists this publication in the National Bibliography;
detailed bibliographic data are available on the Internet at http://dnb.dnb.de .

This book is copyright material and must not be copied, reproduced, transferred,
distributed, leased, licensed or publicly performed or used in any way except as
specifically permitted in writing by the publishers, as allowed under the terms and
conditions under which it was purchased or as strictly permitted by applicable
copyright law. Any unauthorized distribution or use of this text may be a direct
infringement of the author s and publisher s rights and those responsible may be
liable in law accordingly.

Imprint:

Copyright © 2009 GRIN Verlag, Open Publishing GmbH
Print and binding: Books on Demand GmbH, Norderstedt Germany
ISBN: 9783640458561

This book at GRIN:

http://www.grin.com/en/e-book/137241/time-and-the-other-in-the-imperialist-dis-
course-of-kipling-and-conrad

Mouloud Siber

Time and the Other in the Imperialist Discourse of Kipling and Conrad

GRIN Publishing

GRIN - Your knowledge has value

Since its foundation in 1998, GRIN has specialized in publishing academic texts by students, college teachers and other academics as e-book and printed book. The website www.grin.com is an ideal platform for presenting term papers, final papers, scientific essays, dissertations and specialist books.

Visit us on the internet:

http://www.grin.com/

http://www.facebook.com/grincom

http://www.twitter.com/grin_com

Introduction

The reinforcement of the colonial contact between the Western powers and the non-Western world in the nineteenth century was accompanied with a large literary canon that represented this encounter. Some of the most pertinent works provided an ideological support for the expansion of the former to the latter. Rudyard Kipling and Joseph Conrad, among others, are considered by many as the canonical examples of this accompaniment. The emergence of this literature has also generated some seminal works in postcolonial theory like Edward Said's *Orientalism* (1978) and *Culture and Imperialism* (1993). In recent years, there has been a large bulk of criticism that has studied these two writers, their colonial discourses and the way they represent the 'Other' in relation to the colonial Self.

To start with Rudyard Kipling, Harris (1992) hints at Kipling's attitude towards the encounter between the British colonists and the Indians. For Harris, Kipling's *Kim* presents India "as a mysterious land in which people believe in magic and witchcraft and in which astrology is widely practiced and used in most important social ceremonies" (Harris, 1992: 20). Besides, Lane (1995) compares the Orient to a child who is unable to take care of himself, hence his need for the authority of the father, who is analogous to Britain.

As for Conrad's interests in the colonial encounter, Griffith (1995) insists on the impact of the exotic environment on the European subjects. Griffith foregrounds the idea that the European subject, once in an exotic land, loses restraint in the face of the unknown and his supposed retreat from 'civilisation'. For instance, he observes that "the theme of the degeneration of the European colonist in the East" (Griffith, 1995: 145) is recurrent in Conrad's fiction. Besides, the fear of the Malayan 'Other' is expressed through his disdain for sexual relationships with native people, which would mean the idea of "going native" (Ibid. 146). Most recently, Hampson (2000) studies Conrad's Malay fiction under the perspective that it is engaged with describing the encounter between the West and the Malay world and showing what it means to be a Westerner in the Malay Archipelago. Some of the most pertinent works by Joseph Conrad and Rudyard Kipling inspire from the writings of other disciplines to provide this support to empire. Not only do they weave with the political theory of the epoch but they inspire from the ethnological and anthropological studies, as well. All of Harris (1992), Lane (1995), Griffith (1995) and Hampson (2000) make reference to issues like the writers' appropriation of Darwinian thought to justify the nineteenth century imperial project. Much has been said about the aspects of their works which make the contrast between the superiority of the Westerner and the inferiority of the non-Western 'Other'. However, the writers' use of *time* is granted no specific attention. Yet, according to Fabian (1983), time has played a significant role in the justification of the imperial project.

Issue and Working Hypothesis

It is the purpose of this paper to explore the issue of time and the 'Other' in the writings of Rudyard Kipling and Joseph Conrad. It aims at showing that both writers use time in such a way as to justify the imperial project and the expansion of the European powers to the territory of the 'Other'. The idea is that they use time from a Darwinian or evolutionary perspective and distinguish between a Western conception of time and a non-Western one. One is *evolutionary* and the other is static or *primitive*, to use Fabian's terms. (Fabian, 2002: 17, 18) These opposed conceptions provide a necessary support for imperial expansion. This idea is all the more interesting to explore in the sense that it inspires from the intellectual and geopolitical discourse of the colonial period in relation to India, the Dark Continent and other conquered parts of the world.

Indeed, in the nineteenth century, some ideas emphasized that the people of India needed to be governed by a superior race. For instance, John Stuart Mill in his essay *Considerations on Representative Government* points out that there exists a hierarchy of societies in the world. At the bottom are societies like India that are "backward", "savage" or "barbaric". These 'backward' societies cannot govern themselves properly (Mill, 1904: 321). This goes without saying that the doctrine of paternalism, which states that the so-called "backward and primitive" societies need the Western world, was contemporary to Kipling's and Conrad's works. In this period, "the 'civilised/ 'savage' ('primitive', 'backward') contrast became a standard element" (Federeci, 1995: 66), a period that is known for its prevalent ideas of the superiority of European civilisation and the "inferiority" of other races. This was reinforced by the ethnographic studies that provided basic argument for the superiority of Western civilisation and the inferiority of other races. Besides, Charles Darwin's theory of evolution and its basic concepts of "natural selection" and the "survival of the fittest" are significant tenets of the era of European imperialism. Along with this intellectual atmosphere, there emerged what Edward Said coins the *consolidating literature of empire*, which provides ideological support for the imperial enterprise, adding to the existing Orientalist discourse. In the meantime, the nineteenth century Western people started to grant much importance to time so that their conception of time became linear and evolutionary. This was the result of the evolutions and revolutions that occurred in different fields like science and industry.

To achieve the study of Kipling's and Conrad's ideological appropriation of time, primary research will be made on Joseph Conrad's *Heart of Darkness*, *Lord Jim* and "Youth" and Rudyard Kipling's *Kim*. As for methodology, reference will be made to Edward Said's *Orientalism* (1978) and Johannes Fabian's *Time and the Other: How Anthropology Makes Its Object* (1983).

Discussion

Rudyard Kipling and Joseph Conrad draw a dichotomy between the Western 'Self' and the colonial 'Other' in such a way as to justify imperialism. In Saidan terms, the two writers adopt a process of *Othering*, which aims at creating the colonial 'Other' as the contrastive image of the colonial 'Self'. They particularly emphasise the superiority of the Westerners and the inferiority of the non-Westerners. One of the most important ideological tools they appropriate for this purpose is the issue of *time*, which they consider mainly from an evolutionary perspective.

In relation to the idea of the evolutionary thought and the concept of time, Kipling stresses the "backwardness" of the Indian people and the advancement of the white races. In fact, he makes a fundamental distinction between two different conceptions of time as it is *perceived* by the Oriental and as it is *conceived* by the European. For the Indians, time has no importance; they do not really accord much economic, social, and even metaphysical importance to it, whereas for the Europeans, time means much more than passage in existence. It has a much more economic, social and intellectual significance. In *Kim*, there is a clear insistence upon the way time is considered by the Indians for whom "all hours of the twenty four are alike" (Kipling, 1994: 40). The Oriental does not really consider the importance of time, so he doesn't care about what he can accomplish in it. He is the one to wait too long to do or to get something because he does not behave in accordance with time, whereas for the European every minute counts much in his daily life. It is thanks to this importance accorded to time that the Europeans attained an advanced existence.

Kipling echoes the nineteenth century evolutionary thought. With the emergence of Darwin's evolutionary thinking, the conception of time became linear and evolutionary. This linearity of time means that it progresses upwards, and the past is unrecoverable. With the linear consideration of time, society progressed quickly, especially with the invention of time-winning machines like the train, which shortened the distance and gained time. In Victorian England, time became very much important in social and economic life. Economic activity was arranged according to time-scales. The working day respected a certain timescale, and there was spare-time which allowed the worker to take rest and enjoy in his hobbies. This is related to the Victorian faith in progress and its ideal of work ethics, which promote the individual and society. Other European societies in which time was of paramount importance advanced easily and quickly. Nonetheless, most of the Oriental societies, which accorded little or no importance to it, remained stationary or backward. This is to say that for Kipling, one of the reasons for the "backwardness" of the Indian society is related to their conception of time. Their "backwardness" legitimates the intervention of Britain. In *Kim*, he stresses the two distinct conceptions of time, the Western and the Oriental, to show that the Orientals need to be impelled to consider time *linearly* rather than *cyclically* and develop a time awareness so as to promote their progress. Consequently, it is no accident that Kipling grants much importance to the train in *Kim*. The English introduced the train to the Indian subcontinent so as shorten the distance and save time for themselves and the Indians, some of whom enjoy in the advantages of this *time* winning machine. It should be said that the large majority of the Indians have no awareness of time; only the privileged few have been influenced by the English to relatively consider the importance of time.

One of the aspects of the lack of time awareness on the part of the Oriental can be related to the Buddhist religion. In Buddhism, time is more related to the metaphysical than to the earthly life, so the Buddhist can spend hours of meditation in order to allow to the 'self' a cosmic relationship with what is beyond nature. In hours of meditation, the Buddhist is cut off from reality. Another instance is related to the Muslim religion and its lack of time awareness. These two religions are important in India, and in *Kim*, the Indians range from Mohammedanism, heathenism or Buddhism. This amounts to say that the religious believes and practices of the Oriental people constitute an obstacle to their advancement because they accord much importance to the metaphysical and tend to neglect space and time, or the *here* and *now* of their society. Fabian (1983) makes a distinction between *sacred* time and *secular* time. The former belongs to the Orientals and the Mediterraneans, whereas the second belongs to the Judeo-Christians. (Fabian, 2002: 2) The sacredness of time for the Orientals is related to their religious practices; what is important to them is to spend as much time as possible on praying and worship. However, for the Westerners, it is rather evolutionary. Their worship is just part of their daily activities. What is all the more interesting is that they use this conception of time for imperial objectives. In attempting to convert the non-Christians, they want to "secularize Judeo-Christian Time by generalizing and universalizing it" (Ibid. 2). Through this aim, the Christian missions basically serve the implementation of Western powers in the non-Western worlds.

Besides, the people Kim meets throughout his journey with the lama are described as 'old' people. This is mainly related to the people of the hills. The adjective 'old' denotes a temporal category which is contrasted to 'young'. One relates to the past, and it is concerned with the Indians. The other relates to the advanced present, and it is concerned with the white race. The Indians as any other Oriental races belong to the beginning of humanity, whereas through the focus put on European progress, one understands the idea of evolution. The most important example which shows the old age of India and the youth of Europe is related to the relationship between the 'old' lama and the 'young' Kim. Their relationship is allegorical of this distinction between primitive time and evolutionary time. The European lives an evolutionary time, so there is a constant renewal and change. By contrast, the Indian lives a static time, so there is no change. The youth of the European is the result of this constant renewal, whereas the old age of the Indian stems from this static state. Allegorically, the former is represented by Kim, whereas the latter is represented by the lama.

It follows that the distinction between the time of the European and that of the Oriental is related to age. The former is young, the latter old. The importance of this distinction is related to the lama's need for Kim. In fact, the relationship between the two is based on mutual interests. The lama benefits from the youth of Kim, and Kim in his turn serves his political aims in travelling with the old lama. In the beginning of the novel, it is maintained that the old lama benefits from the youth of Kim. Kim's benefit from this friendship is related to his need to discover the truth around his father's prophecy of the "Red Bull in a greed field". This is directly political since Kim discovers that as a white boy he has much political power in the Indian subcontinent. This friendship is allegorical of the British Rule in India. On the one hand, it shows the service done by the British in India. On the other hand, it displays the idea of domination. The fate of the Indians, it seems, is to be subjected to the power of the white man in view of their primitivism and the modernity of the white man. It means that the relationship between the lama and Kim is a relationship of domination as any other relationship between the European and his Other, and time is ideologically used to promote this domination.

As for Conrad's narratives, it is undeniable that Conrad uses time in an ideological way to support European expansion. In fact, like Rudyard Kipling's opposition between the European conception of time and the Oriental one, he distinguishes between the time of the Europeans and that of their "Others". The former belong to present, which is the highest point in the evolutionary ladder, whereas the latter belong to the past. They are still in the beginning of existence, so they have no awareness of the passage of time. By contrast, the Europeans have taken long steps forward in time. Their belongingness to the present is characterised by their awareness of the passage of time and their desire to progress as time moves forward, hence their technical, scientific and artistic *achievements*. In *Heart of Darkness*, Marlow emphasises these ideas when he speaks of a group of natives being employed by the Europeans. Marlow says,

> They had been engaged for six months (I don't think a single one of them had any clear idea of time as we at the end countless ages. They still belonged to the beginnings of time – had no inherited experience to teach them as it were

> (Conrad, 1983: 75)

From the aforementioned quote, there is a clear contrast between the static time of the African people and the evolutionary one of the Europeans. Conrad insists on the idea that the Africans are as they were in the beginning of existence; there is no evolution. In the words of Edward Said, colonial discourse emphasises the idea that the "great moments [of Europe's Others] were in the past" (Said, 1995: 35).

Besides, from the above there is the use of the personal pronouns *they* and *we*, which emphasises Conrad's distinction between Europe and its 'Others'. Edward Said observes that the use of the personal pronouns *we* and *they* and their objective forms *us* and *them* is the first sign of a typical Orientalist attitude which separates between the Western superior coloniser and the colonised 'Other'. For instance, *we* stands for "'the English', for whom the pronoun 'we' is used with the full weight of a distinguished powerful man who feels himself to be representative of all that is best in his nation's history". *They* stands for all Orientals who are "a subject race, dominated by a race that knows them and what is good for them better than they could possibly know themselves" (Said, 1995: 34-35).

The majority of Conrad's narratives insist upon the primitivism and savagery of the African and Oriental people. The words savagery and primitivism, which are associated to the non-Westerners, are two *temporal* words that abound in Conrad's texts to distinguish them from the civilised white man. The word *savagery* according to Fabian (1983) "denotes a stage in a developmental sequence [and it] is a marker of the past" (Fabian, 2002: 75). Speaking about the African people Marlow meets in the Kurtz's station, he says,

> I noticed that the crowd of *savages* was vanishing without any perceptible retreat, as if the forest that had ejected these beings so suddenly had drawn them in again as the breath in a long aspiration.

> (Conrad, 1983: 99; italics mine)

Not only do these "savages" belong to the forest but they belong to the past as well, the past which is of course symbolised by the forest, for the forest bears no mark of change and development. One understands from the above that these "savages" do not have a place in the history annals nor do they know about the remaining world. They live in a world of their own, where civilisation does not penetrate. They live an anonymous life of their own, and they communicate in a way of their own but which has nothing do with the human language for the European imperialists. Similarly, in "An Outpost of Progress", they are reduced to the status of "howling savages" that "made an uncouth babbling noise when they spoke, moved in a stately manner, and sent quick, wild glances out of their startled, never-resting eyes" (Conrad, 1990: 9).

Besides, one feels Conrad's appropriation of time in "Youth", where he attributes the Malays and the whole East a primitive state. "This was the East of ancient navigators, so old so mysterious, resplendent and sombre, living and unchanged", he says (Conrad, 1990: 130). In terms of time, Conrad's description implies the idea that the East and its people are static. They have not changed from the same *primitive state* as when they were encountered by the first ancient European explorers. It means that the Easterners do not progress or evolve. Accordingly, they "[live] in another Time" (Fabian, 2008: 27). By contrast, the Europeans have taken a very long step forward ever since the first explorers had reached the East. In fact, contrary to the Easterners, the Westerners have reached the highest point of human development since their conception of time is evolutionary and linear. The Western man never looks backward, hence his progress. The majority of the Westerners in the end of the nineteenth and early twentieth centuries believed that time moved forward, and its move "accomplished or brought about things in the course of evolution […] theirs was a preoccupation with stages leading to civilization" (Fabian, 2002: 15).

In *Lord Jim*, the description of the *Patna* also denotes an ideological use of time. It is depicted as "a local steamer as **old as the hills**, lean like greyhound, and eaten up with rust worse than a condemned water-tank" (Conrad, 1994: 16-17; emphasis mine). The temporal adjective *old* denotes the past, which mainly means that the *Patna* belongs to the past. Conrad uses the *Patna* as a metaphor to stand for the Orient. This can be understood through the idea that "She was owned by a Chinaman, charted by an Arab, and commanded by a sort of renegade New South Wales German […] eight hundred pilgrims (more or less) were driven on board of her" (Ibid. 17). It means that its occupants are mostly Orientals headed by a white man. The idea that the ship is old and rusty is meaningful of the primitivism of the Orient. It also suggests the idea of the superiority of the West and the inferiority of the Orient. This can be explained by the calamity that befalls upon the ship in its course to Jedah, which is attributed to its old age and rust. Were it a Western steamer the calamity would not befall upon her since the Western ships are modern.

Conrad's appropriation of time is all the more important in the second part of *Lord Jim.* When Marlow departs from Patusan to England, he says

> But next morning, at the first bend of the river shutting off the houses of Patusan, all this dropped out of my sight bodily, with its colour, its design, and its meaning, like a picture created by fancy on a canvas, upon which, after long contemplation, you turn your back for the last time. It remains in the memory motionless, unfaded with its life arrested, in an unchanging light. […] I had turned away from the picture and was going back to the world where events move, men change, light flickers, life flows in a clear stream, no matter whether mud or over stones.   (Conrad, 1994: 248)

One clearly understands the contrast between two worlds: the static Orient and the constantly changing West or Europe. Marlow leaves a world that does in no way know change through time to a world on the move as time progresses.

Another parallel issue which Conrad pays attention to is the Victorian notion that "primitive" people lacked a history. This idea of the people without history is an imperial ideology that sought to ease the conquest of other people. In *Heart of Darkness,* this ideology is given voice. This can be attributed to the idea that Marlow's journey involves a voyage to the earliest beginning of time, to prehistory. "We were wanderers on a prehistoric earth, on an earth that wore the aspect of an unknown planet" (Conrad, 1983: 68), says Marlow, who insists upon this idea. His journey involves a journey to prehistory when man could not yet communicate linguistically – "howling savages" – to have any history of their own. The "howling savages" have no oral tradition to mark it through time, any more than a written one to engrave it. They have nothing to record because they are like animals that live for living's sake. It means that Conrad excludes the African people from historical development in the same way as Hegel does for the non- Western world. Indeed, Hegel elaborates a "hierarchical scheme to describe the place of the Western world in historical development" (Federeci, 1995: 67). His ideas on history are related to his belief that history runs unilaterally from East to West, or from South to North and progresses and develops as it goes forwards. This means that the place of the non-West in history is a primitive one, whereas that of the West is progressive and civilised. Hegel bases his argument on the idea that the Western people achieved a higher stage of reason and understanding as opposed to the non-Western people who are supposedly "backward" rather progressive.

Conclusion

It follows that the writings of Joseph Conrad and Rudyard Kipling appropriate *time* as an ideological tool so as to provide primary support for the British Empire. This is achieved by the dichotomy they draw between the primitivism of the non-Western people and the progress and modernity of the Westerners. They show that the former need the intervention of the latter so as to promote their progress and get them out of their primitivism. The two writers make some polyphonic appeal to other disciplines so as to achieve this purpose. Therefore, they, for instance, weave their texts with the teachings of anthropology, biology and history, hence the importance they grant to the concept of *time* as it is viewed in the evolutionary thought of the nineteenth century. They do this by the dichotomy they draw between the *primitive time* of the non-Western people and the *evolutionary time* of the Westerners.

Perhaps it is pertinent an attempt to draw a parallel with contemporary political discourse and the way, for instance, Africa is regarded by politicians in the West. Indeed, one of the prominent world leaders of the time is the French president Nicholas Sarkozy. In his Dakar discourse of July 26, 2007, he addresses to the African nations with a *quasi* dominative tone. One of the ideas he sustains is related to the dichotomy drawn between *time* in the West and *time* in the non-West, saying that the African man differs from the Westerner in that the former "vit avec les saisons, dont l'idéal de vie est d'être en harmonie avec la nature, ne connaît que l'éternel recommencement du temps rythmé par la répétition sans fin des mêmes gestes et des mêmes paroles." (Sarkozy, 2007) The idea is that for Sarkozy as for Rudyard Kipling, Joseph Conrad and many others, the African man has always had a cyclical rather than an evolutionary conception of time, which results in his underdevelopment and dependence since there is no progress.

Works Cited

Conrad, Joseph (1994). *Lord Jim*. London: Penguin Books, 1900.

-----. (1983) *Heart of Darkness*. Harmondsworth: Penguin Classics, 1902.

-----. (1990) *Heart of Darkness and Other Tales*. Ed. Cedric Watts. Oxford: Oxford University Press.

Kipling, Rudyard (1994). *Kim*. London: Penguin Popular Classics, 1901.

Griffith, John W. (1995) *Joseph Conrad and the Anthropological Dilemma: 'Bewildered Travellers'*. Oxford: Oxford University Press.

Fabian, Johannes. (2002) *Time and the Other: How Anthropology Makes its Object*. New York: Columbia University Press, 1983.

Federici, Silvia, Ed. (1995) *Enduring Western Civilization: The Construction of the Concept of Western Civilization and Its "Others"*. Westport: Praeger.

Hampson, Robert (2000). *Cross-cultural Encounters in Joseph Conrad's Malay Fiction*. New York: Palgrave.

Harris, Michael (1992). *Outsiders and Insiders: Perspectives in Third World Culture in British and Post-Colonial Fiction*. New York: Peter Lang Publishing, Inc.

Lane, Christopher (1995). *The Ruling Passion: British Colonial Allegory and the Paradox of Homosexual Desire*. Durham: Duke University Press.

Mill, John Stuart (1904). *Considerations on Representative Government*. New York: The New Universal Library, 1861.

Said, Edward W. (1994). *Culture and Imperialism*. London: Vintage, 1993.

Said, Edward W (1995). *Orientalism: Western Conceptions of the Orient*. London: Penguin Books, 1978.

Sarkozy, Nicholas (2007). « Allocution de M. Nicolas SARKOZY, Président de la République, prononcée à l'Université de Dakar ». [Online] Available: http://www.elysee.fr/elysee/elysee.fr/francais/interventions/2007/juillet/allocution_a_l_universite_de_dakar.79184.html (Accessed on August 2009)

YOUR KNOWLEDGE HAS VALUE

- We will publish your bachelor's and master's thesis, essays and papers

- Your own eBook and book - sold worldwide in all relevant shops

- Earn money with each sale

Upload your text at www.GRIN.com and publish for free